THE 1001 IDEAS BLANK PAPER SKETCHBOOK FOR INNOVATIVE CREATIVES

ISBN: 978-3-9503878-5-8

Publisher: serendii publishing, Austria
DREAMICON VALLEY

(serendii)

www.ingramcontent.com/pod-product-compliance
Lightning Source LLC
Chambersburg PA
CBHW060301010526
44108CB00042B/2593
9783950387858